THE COMPLETE
BOOK OF
QUESTIONS

Other Resources by Garry Poole

Seeker Small Groups
The Three Habits of Highly Contagious Christians

In the Tough Questions Series:

Don't All Religions Lead to God?
How Could God Allow Suffering and Evil?
How Does Anyone Know God Exists?
Why Become a Christian?
Tough Questions Leader's Guide (with Judson Poling)

1001 | Conversation Starters for Any Occasion

THE COMPLETE BOOK OF QUESTIONS

GARRY POOLE

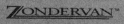

ZONDERVAN™

GRAND RAPIDS, MICHIGAN 49530 USA

WILLOW CREEK RESOURCES

We want to hear from you. Please send your comments about
this book to us in care of zreview@zondervan.com. Thank you.

ZONDERVAN™

The Complete Book of Questions
Copyright © 2003 by Willow Creek Association

Requests for information should be addressed to:

Zondervan, *Grand Rapids, Michigan 49530*

ISBN: 0-310-24420-X

Interior design by Tracey Moran

Printed in the United States of America

03 04 05 06 07 08 09 /❖ DC/ 10 9 8 7 6 5 4 3 2 1

To Jim Poole and Rosanne Vale
who endured their older brother's
relentless barrage of questions
and inspired a constant stream of new ones

ACKNOWLEDGMENTS

It is better to know some of the questions than all of the answers.

—James Thurber

It seems like there are those who have all the answers and others who have only questions. And unless you're lucky, it's a rare thing to stumble across people with a healthy dose of both questions and answers.

I'm very lucky.

My brother Jim Poole is simply a creative genius. He's a witty wordsmith with an uncanny sense of what's what. Thanks for your astute observations and handing over all your great ideas.

My colleague Laura Allen is a talented mastermind. She's a "walking thesaurus" with a heart of gold.

Thanks for sharing your wealth of wisdom and keen insights.

Thanks, Jim and Laura, for inspiring me to take this book to the next level and your willingness to go above and beyond time after time.

My mother, Barbara Poole, and friend Judy Keene supplied lots of suggestions and polished the manuscript. Thanks for your contributions and edits—they were all good ones.

And a special thanks to all my friends and family members who over the years have kindled these 1001 questions—and illuminated their answers.

The answer, my friend, is blowin' in the wind.

—*Bob Dylan*

INTRODUCTION

*Can I ask you
a question?*

—*Socrates*

The Power of Questions

Questions are great conversation starters. It seems everyone has a story to tell or an opinion to share. And to get it, you need only to ask. Good questions invite people to open up about themselves and divulge their thoughts and feelings on a wide variety of topics. They're the secret behind getting acquainted with someone you have recently met or learning something completely new about someone you've known for years. If you learn to pose the right questions, you'll gain a better understanding of who your friends are and what makes them tick.

Don't you appreciate it when someone asks *you* sincere questions? It conveys an interest in your opinions and insights. It demonstrates a desire to know who you are and what you really think. And that means a lot. There is something powerful about questions that force you to think, look within yourself, examine your heart, and search for answers. And it's in the process of responding to those questions that you often make discoveries about yourself—things you never even realized before.

Questions also function remarkably well in the context of discussion groups. They draw group participants into the dialogue—less outspoken individuals are coaxed out of their shells and more talkative types are reigned in to focus on the issue at hand. Asking great questions in a group setting is the quickest and easiest way to spark stimulating discussions.

1001 Questions

But even though most of us realize the importance of raising questions, asking good ones is sometimes another matter. They are not always that simple to think up. That's where *The Complete Book of Questions* comes in! This book is one big compilation of questions—1001 questions you can use in just about any context to launch great conversations. And many of these questions are likely to trigger other questions you may also wish to discuss. Think of this book as a tool to spark interaction—to know and understand others, and yourself, better.

All of the questions in this book have been divided into ten categories for easy reference. Some questions, of course, might readily fit into multiple categories, so this is just one way to sort them. The box below gives a short description of each category of questions:

Questions	Category	Description
1–100	**Light & Easy**	Simple, light-hearted topics
101–200	**Personal Profile**	Personality traits and behaviors
201–300	**Preferences**	Likes and dislikes, favorites
301–400	**Blast from the Past**	Past personal experiences
401–500	**Just Imagine**	Speculation and imagination
501–600	**Viewpoints**	Opinions and perspectives
601-700	**Hard-Hitting**	Deep and challenging themes
701–800	**From the Heart**	Feelings and emotions
801–900	**Spiritually Speaking**	Basic spiritual subjects
901–1001	**Extreme Spiritual Matters**	Complex spiritual issues

Guidelines

Since this is a book full of questions, no answers are provided. That's where you and your friends and family members step in! As you use these questions to interact with one another, remember there are no right or wrong answers. Don't feel pressured to respond in any certain way—just be yourself and be true to who you are. Here are a few additional guidelines to keep in mind:

- Most of the questions are "open-ended" (seeking expanded responses), while others are "closed-ended" (calling for short, one-word answers). In either case, develop your answer as little or as much as you feel comfortable doing.

- In the rare case you find a question that is irrelevant or not something you wish to answer, simply skip it and pick another one.

- The first several categories of questions are the most nonthreatening and, therefore, the easiest to answer. These are the best ones to use with new acquaintances.

- The last few categories contain questions of a deeper nature, which may best be utilized in settings where you know the other participants fairly well and are ready to tackle issues of greater significance.

- The Spiritually Speaking category lists questions that address very basic spiritual issues, while the Extreme Spiritual Matters section includes questions that will stretch and challenge you on your personal spiritual journey.

Applications

There are probably as many ways to put this book to use as there are questions within it! So be creative. Experiment with a variety of methods to apply these questions in different contexts. To get you started, consider the following ideas:

- Whether you're with one other individual or a whole group of people, use this book to spark conversations in different settings and occasions: social and holiday gatherings, road trips, meals, dates, discussion groups, family times, vacations, etc.

- Randomly select a number, read that question, and answer it. Take turns, inviting each person to pick a different number—or, if someone prefers, let him or her answer a question that was previously chosen.

- Limit the questions to be selected to one specific category—or two or three categories. Or open up the options to include each and every question in the book.

- Predetermine one particular question—or several of them—you'd like everyone in your group to answer.

- If you're in a discussion group, look for relevant questions to use as icebreakers and to supplement your topic of discussion.

Listen Well

Finally, as important as good questions are, nothing compares to the significance of developing the skill of effectively *listening* to one another. Can you think of a time when a person turned to face you squarely and displayed a sincere desire to fully hear and understand you? Chances are, that kind of undivided attention made quite an impact on you. Even though it might be tempting to think instead about how you would respond to a given question, do your best to listen well enough to really *understand* each other.

As you explore these 1001 questions, make the most of the conversations that ensue. Share your responses openly and listen intently to one another. In so doing, you'll express unselfish candor and respect, which will go a long way toward taking your relationships to a whole new level. Now that's a gift you can treasure!

LIGHT & EASY

1. Do you squeeze the toothpaste tube or roll it? What's the advantage of your method?

2. How many siblings do you have? What's your birth order?

3. What's something you've won and how did you win it?

4. What's one of your nicknames? What do you prefer to be called?

5. What's something your parents used to say to you as a child that you promised yourself you'd never say—but now you catch yourself saying all the time?

6. What's something you intended to do today, but didn't? Why not?

7. Using only one word per person, what was your first impression of each person present with you now?

8. What's something that people do in traffic that really bothers you?

9. Who is the closest friend you've ever had? Describe that relationship.

10. What books on your shelf are begging to be read?

11. What room in your house best reflects your personality? Explain why.

12. How often do you doodle? What do your doodles usually look like?

13. What do you do if you can't sleep at night? Do you count sheep, toss and turn, or get up and try to do something productive?

14. Which do you do more often: hum or whistle? Hum or whistle your answer.

15. What animal are you the most like? Why?

16. How many days could you last in solitary confinement? How would you do it?

17. Do you save old greeting cards and letters, or throw them all away? Why?

18. On a scale of 1 to 10, how well do you sing?

19. When you're alone at home, do you wear shoes, socks, slippers, or go barefoot?

20. What are the advantages and disadvantages of being your height?

21. When was the last picnic you went on? Describe it.

22. How many discount or savings coupons do you clip in an average month? How many expire before you use them?

23. Who's the biggest "pack rat" you know?

24. Whose autographs have you collected?

25. What's something you should throw away, but can't? Explain.

26. What food items did you eat so far today?

27. How often do you get a haircut? Describe your worst haircut.

28. How particular are you about the mainte-
    nance of your car?

29. Who's the most famous person you have ever
    met? What famous person would you most
    like to meet?

30. What is your most unusual nighttime or
    morning ritual?

31. How often do you read your horoscope? Do
    you believe there's any truth to it?

32. What kinds of movies do you most enjoy?
    Why?

33. When was the last time you stubbed your
    toe so hard it brought tears to your eyes?

34. How do you get rid of pesky phone calls
    from telemarketers?

35. What are you a "natural" at doing?

36. What's the story behind a time when you
    got locked out?

37. When's the last time you had to give a speech? How did it go?

38. How often do you get sick?

39. What's something valuable that you accidentally dropped and broke? Describe the situation.

40. What's the first thing that comes to mind when you hear the word "fun"?

41. At amusement parks, are you drawn more to the scariest roller coaster or the tamest merry-go-round? Why?

42. When's the last time you square-danced or line-danced? Rate your dancing ability on a scale of 1 to 10.

43. What are some of the wildest animals you've ever touched?

44. How many hours do you spend on your computer each day? How much time do you spend "surfing the Web"?

45. What makes you tick?

46. What has been your best work of art? Describe it.

47. What is something mischievous you have done?

48. When you leave a room, do you turn the lights off behind you or keep the lights on throughout your house most of the time? Explain your answer.

49. What's the worst tasting thing you've ever eaten?

50. When talking to someone while standing, are your arms usually at your sides, in your pockets, crossed in front of you, or gesturing descriptively? Demonstrate your answer.

51. What magazines do you subscribe to, and how many of those do you actually read or look through? Do you throw any of them away unread?

52. Have you ever purchased anything from a telemarketer? If so, what was it? If not, why didn't you?

53. How frequently do you purchase lottery tickets or mail in sweepstakes registrations? Have you ever won anything from them?

54. What's the best New Year's resolution you've ever made?

55. When making an entrance into a social gathering, do you make your presence known so everyone notices you, slip in and look for someone you know, or sneak in as quietly as possible and find a safe spot to hide? Why?

56. How many hours a week do you watch TV? Is that too little, too much, or just enough?

57. What's your favorite kind of candy?

58. What's your strongest sense?

59. Are you most likely to finish your taxes as soon as you receive your W–2s or as close to April 15 as possible? How many times have you filed for an extension?

60. What can your friends predict you will grumble about most?

61. Do you prefer keeping the television channel remote in hand or giving it up? Why?

62. How many times a day do you look at yourself in the mirror?

63. When you travel, do you pack too much or too little? Explain.

64. What's the wackiest belief you held as a child?

65. What's your favorite beverage?

66. What are the best steps you've ever taken in an effort to improve your health?

67. When relaxing on the floor, do you sit cross-legged, fold your legs to one side, sit with your legs straight out in front of you, or recline?

68. Have you ever been an audience member for any television shows? Which ones? For which ones would you like to be an audience member?

69. What's one fashion trend you hope never comes back? Which ones have come back that you wish hadn't?

70. What magic tricks do you know? Perform one now.

71. What's the best (or funniest) commercial you've ever seen?

72. When was the last time you sat on a park bench for more than ten minutes? Describe the occasion.

73. What's the most embarrassing thing you've seen someone else do?

74. When something is funny, do you usually laugh raucously, hiss, snort, chuckle quietly to yourself, or smile and nudge the person next to you?

75. How important is it to you that people remember, spell, and pronounce your name correctly? Why?

76. What's your favorite item to cook? Why?

77. Do you usually send serious or humorous greeting cards? Why?

78. Would you ever be interested in observing a surgery or do you turn away when the nurse brings out the needle? Why?

79. Which movies have you watched over and over again?

80. What do you admire most about your best friend?

81. What was one vacation that lasted too long?

82. To feel rested, how many hours of sleep do you need each night?

83. What's one guilty pleasure you enjoy too much to give up?

84. Who performs more random acts of kindness than anyone else you know? Give the details.

85. What jingle comes to your mind? Hum or whistle it right now and see if others can correctly guess it!

86. How many credit cards do you have? How often do you use them?

87. How often do you leisurely eat a meal with friends?

88. Who's the jolliest person you know? Describe him or her.

89. What sound drives you crazy?

90. What sound lulls you to sleep?

91. Who's the smartest person you know?

92. What food do you eat for comfort?

93. How often do you read the newspaper? Which sections do you turn to first?

94. In one sentence, how would you describe your best friend?

95. How long, on average, does it take you to fall asleep once you turn out the lights?

96. What items do you currently have stored in the trunk of your car?

97. Which animals scare you most? Why?

98. What remedy for curing the common cold works best for you?

99. Where are you ticklish? How much does it bother you to be tickled?

100. Is the paper money in your possession right now organized sequentially according to denomination and with the bills right side up and facing the same way? Why or why not?

PERSONAL PROFILE

101. Are you a hugger or a non-hugger? Why?

102. What drives you crazy?

103. Are you serious-minded or a jokester? Why?

104. Are you more likely to avoid conflict or engage in it head-on? Why?

105. What was the most recent compliment you received and savored?

106. What's something about yourself that you hope will change, but that probably never will?

107. What's something about yourself that you hope will never change?

108. Are you a leader or a follower? How do you know?

109. Are you more of a rule breaker or a rule keeper? Why?

110. Would you describe yourself as an extrovert or an introvert? Give an example.

111. Would you describe yourself as more of a feeler or a thinker? Why?

112. Are you usually late, early, or on time? Why?

113. What goals have you recently set for yourself, and how are you doing on them so far?

114. To what degree are you patriotic? How do you express your patriotism?

115. Are you a creature of habit? Explain your answer.

116. In what situations are you most likely to procrastinate?

117. What books have made a big impact on you?

118. At what age do you hope to retire? Explain.

119. How much of a bargain hunter are you? Explain.

120. How much of a shopper are you? Where's your favorite place to shop?

121. Are you ever a high-maintenance person? Explain.

122. When was the last time you really pushed yourself to your physical limits? Explain.

123. What's one of your hobbies?

124. How much poetry have you written in your life?

125. How do you typically react in a sudden, extreme, pressure-filled crisis?

126. How do you go about illuminating "blind spots" in your life?

127. How mechanically inclined do you consider yourself? Give an example.

128. How many different conversations can you adequately carry on at the same time?

129. Are you a person who has a whole lot of acquaintances or just a few very close friends? Why?

130. How comfortable are you with uncertainty? Explain.

131. On a scale of 1 to 10, how computer savvy are you? Explain.

132. Are you superstitious? Give an example.

133. What one word best describes your mother?

134. What one word best describes your father?

135. Do you have a collection? If so, what do you collect and why?

136. When are you shy?

137. Do you tend to save everything or toss everything? Why?

138. What's something you regret losing, selling, or giving away? Explain why.

139. How absentminded do you get? Give an example.

140. Which is better: your short-term or your long-term memory?

141. What's your idea of cute?

142. Are you more inclined to "build your own empire" or "unleash the potential of others"? Explain.

143. What do you take for granted the most?

144. How often do you interrupt others while they are talking? Give a reason for your answer.

145. When you have nothing pressing, where does your mind drift?

146. What are your career goals?

147. How competitive are you? Explain.

148. Are you a penny-pincher or a big spender? Why?

149. Would you describe yourself as more laid back or more intense? Why?

150. Are you a risk taker? Why or why not?

151. Do you care more about pleasing people or speaking the truth? Explain your answer.

152. What inspires you to write?

153. What big challenge have you taken on recently?

154. When was the last time you wanted to scream? Explain.

155. Do you ever double or triple check things? If so, what?

156. What bores you?

157. What's someone's idiosyncrasy that really bothers you?

158. What's an idiosyncrasy or strange habit that you have?

159. On a scale of 1 to 10, how controlling a person are you? Explain.

160. What bad habit do you wish you could break?

161. On a scale of 1 to 10, how much of a perfectionist are you? Explain.

162. What's a strange occurrence you've observed but, until now, have never (or rarely) shared with anyone?

163. Where do you think you spend most of your money?

164. What do you think about more than anything else?

165. What books are you reading these days?

166. What allergies do you have?

167. How tolerant a person are you?

168. To what extent do others' beliefs influence you? Why?

169. To what degree do you consider yourself athletic? At which sports do you excel?

170. What causes you to get flustered?

171. At what time of the day do you feel your best?

172. What time do you usually wake up in the morning? Do you awaken naturally or need an alarm?

173. What fear would you like to overcome?

174. When do you most feel like a slave to time?

175. What do you consider your best quality?

176. Are you more task oriented or people oriented? Why?

177. How do you feel about your age?

178. Is it more important to you to look good or feel good? Explain.

179. What's your idea of a good time?

180. Are you a compulsive shopper or do you bring a list and carefully consider your purchases? Why?

181. Who is the first person you tell when something good happens to you?

182. Whom do you run to when something bad happens in your life?

183. In what circumstances do your motor skills short-circuit your verbal skills, and vice versa?

184. In what situations are you most uncomfortable?

185. When are you the most at ease with yourself?

186. How good are you at multitasking? Give an example.

187. What do you do when you want to relax?

188. Are you an early bird or a night owl? Why?

189. What's something that amazes you?

190. Do you say "goodbye" quickly, slowly, or not at all? Why?

191. What spells adventure for you?

192. What tests the limits of your sense of balance?

193. How much of a "people watcher" are you? In what places do you find yourself "people watching"?

194. What do you like and dislike most about your current job?

195. Whom do you call when you need a hand?

196. What is your greatest physical challenge?

197. Under what circumstances is it impossible for you to sleep?

198. How do you best avoid conflict?

199. How accident-prone are you? Describe a recent incident.

200. What's the most important thing about you?

PREFERENCES

201. What's your favorite ice-cream brand and flavor?

202. What's your all-time favorite meal, and how often do you enjoy it?

203. What's your all-time favorite movie, and how many times have you seen it?

204. What's your dream job?

205. When you need to confront someone, would you rather communicate in person, on the phone, by e-mail, or by letter? Why?

206. Which do you prefer: the hustle and bustle of city life or the quiet and serenity of country life? Why?

207. Do you read or study best in silence or in a place with background noise? Why?

208. Do you prefer exercising your mind or your body? How frequently do you do either?

209. Do you prefer that people shoot straight with you or carefully temper their words? Why?

210. Are you more of a dog person or a cat person? Why?

211. What's your preference: plane, train, boat, automobile, horse, or camel?

212. How far in advance do you prefer to plan? Why?

213. What's your favorite board game? Do you usually win?

214. Who's your favorite talk show host?

215. Are you a traveler or a homebody? Explain.

216. Do you enjoy a good debate or prefer keeping the peace?

217. What was your favorite recess activity: Dodgeball, Kickball, Four Square, Hopscotch, Freeze Tag, or jump rope?

218. What's your favorite room in your home? Why?

219. Where's your perfect dream vacation spot?

220. Where's your favorite place to take out-of-town guests?

221. Do you prefer to thoroughly deliberate options or decisively draw conclusions? Why?

222. What is your favorite style of music, and how often do you listen to it?

223. What's your pick: hang glide, sky dive, bungee jump, hot air balloon, or kite?

224. Which of the five senses do you treasure most? Why?

225. When you find yourself in an argument, do you prefer to leave and resolve it later or stay and settle it right away? Why?

226. What's one thing you would rather pay someone to do than do yourself? Why?

227. What's one book you recommend and why?

228. What annoys you most about women?

229. What annoys you most about men?

230. What do you like most about women?

231. What do you like most about men?

232. What's your favorite genre of literature?

233. What's your preferred method of getting the news?

234. What's your favorite color? Why?

235. What's your favorite question to ask? What's your favorite question to answer?

236. What's your favorite expression?

237. What's your all-time favorite video game?

238. What real person, dead or alive, do you wish you could be more like? Why?

239. What's your all-time favorite band, and what would you give to meet them?

240. What's your least favorite thing to do? Why?

241. What's your favorite subject to discuss? Why?

242. When you fly, do you prefer to arrive at the airport extra early or get there just in the nick of time? Why?

243. Whom do you most admire? Why?

244. What bothers you most about perfectionists?

245. How do you prefer to give constructive criticism? Do you typically wait for someone to ask for it or not? Why?

246. What are your three favorite television shows? How frequently do you watch them?

247. Of all the tools and gadgets you own, which one do you most enjoy using?

248. What is one of your favorite souvenirs brought back from your travels? Where do you keep it?

249. What's your choice: baseball, football, Frisbee, Hacky Sack, or boomerang?

250. What are the best and worst sounds in the world?

251. When you go to a movie, do you like to sit in the back, middle, or front? Why?

252. Where's your favorite spot from which to view the sunrise or sunset?

253. What's your most and least preferred forms of exercise? Explain.

254. Growing up, what was your favorite fairy tale or children's story? Why?

255. What's your choice: jigsaw, crossword, or numeric puzzles?

256. What is your favorite bumper sticker or t-shirt slogan?

257. What's your favorite aroma or fragrance?

258. What's your favorite spectator sport, and how often do you watch it?

259. What's one of your favorite summer activities to do with family or friends?

260. Do you prefer to plan your vacation or be spontaneous? Why?

261. What's your pleasure: horseshoes, shuffle-board, croquet, archery, or darts?

262. What are your favorite summer and winter sports?

263. What's your most treasured piece of jewelry? Why?

264. What's your reaction toward people who are outspoken about their beliefs? What conditions cause you to dislike or, conversely, enjoy talking with them?

265. What is something that bothers you if it is not done perfectly? Why is that so?

266. Who is your favorite musician, and how often have you seen him or her perform?

267. Who's your favorite comedian?

268. What's your fancy: bird watching, butterfly collecting, flower hunting, shell gathering, or star gazing?

269. What's your favorite fast-food restaurant and how often do you go there?

270. What's the name of your favorite magazine? What do you like most about it?

271. What's the worst movie you've ever seen, and who did you see it with?

272. When driving, are you more likely to listen to the radio, to CDs and tapes, or nothing at all? Why?

273. What's your fancy: skateboard, roller blades, roller skates, ice skates, or snowboard?

274. What's your preferred way to meet new people? Explain.

275. Where's your favorite place to be? Why?

276. How do you prefer to learn or memorize new information?

277. What's your pleasure: tennis, badminton, volleyball, racquetball, or Ping-Pong?

278. What is your favorite day of the week? Why?

279. What's your favorite season of the year? Why?

280. When you are home alone, do you need the stereo, radio, or TV turned on? Or do you prefer the quiet? Explain.

281. What's your preference: wrestling, martial arts, boxing, or fencing?

282. Do you have a set place for everything at home or do you simply let things stay wherever they land? Give some examples.

283. Who's the best cook you know, and what's his or her specialty?

284. Who's the most creative or artistic person you know?

285. What's your preference: motorcycle, dirt bike, moped, mountain bike, racing bike, scooter, or unicycle?

286. What is your favorite poem or saying? Why is it your favorite?

287. What's your favorite quote? Why is it special to you?

288. Do you prefer window or aisle?

289. As you fall asleep, do you prefer to be flat on your back, curled on your side, or on your stomach? What position are you in when you wake up?

290. What type of museum do you most like to visit?

291. What strikes your fancy: zoo, circus, carnival, county fair, or parade?

292. What's your preference: cruise ship, powerboat, sailboat, rowboat, kayak, or inner tube?

293. What's your favorite holiday tradition? What meaning does it have for you?

294. Where's your favorite place to go when you want to be alone? Why?

295. Do you remember jokes very well? What's the best joke you've heard recently?

296. Who's your favorite person in the whole wide world? Why?

297. What's your all-time favorite town or city? Why?

298. Do you have a favorite painting or drawing? What makes it special to you?

299. What social issue fires you up?

300. What are the top three qualities that first
draw you to someone new?

BLAST
FROM ᴛʜᴇ PAST

301. What's one of your greatest achievements?

302. What's your favorite birthday memory?

303. Who was your best friend in high school, and where is he or she now?

304. What was your first job? How much did you get paid?

305. As a kid, what did you want to grow up to be?

306. What photos do you cherish from the past? Where do you keep them now?

307. Was there ever a time when it turned out you were right, in spite of many others who thought otherwise? Explain the situation.

308. What one word sums up your high school experience?

309. When was the last time you played hooky? Explain the situation.

310. As a child, what was your idea of fun?

311. When have you experienced poor customer service? How did you react?

312. What do you remember about your first day of school or your first teacher?

313. What's your most memorable (good or bad) airplane flight?

314. How many bones have you broken? Share the details.

315. What's something you've done that surprised even you?

316. How many times have you had stitches, and what were the circumstances? Explain.

317. What pets did you have growing up? What were their names?

318. Have you ever seen or called a psychic? What was your experience like?

319. Was school easy or difficult for you? How so?

320. What kind of kids did you hang out with in high school?

321. Who was your favorite teacher growing up, and what did you like most about him or her?

322. What is the best bargain you ever found?

323. What's your most treasured heirloom?

324. Can you remember the address of one of your childhood homes? If so, what was it?

325. How have your priorities changed over time? Explain.

326. When did you get your first traffic ticket? Share the details.

327. What's the most dangerous situation you've encountered? How did you react?

328. How did someone plan a surprise for you? What was your reaction?

329. What was your favorite subject in school? Why?

330. Who has made the biggest impact on you? Explain.

331. Who has been your friend the longest? How and when did you meet him or her?

332. Did you or someone you know ever talk a police officer out of writing a ticket? Describe the situation.

333. Growing up, for which holidays did your family decorate the house?

334. Have you ever helped a total stranger? If so, how?

335. Growing up, what was your favorite comic strip?

336. What was an act of kindness you offered or received?

337. Have you dreamed of flying, falling, or running? Describe your most vivid memory of one of these dreams.

338. Have you ever had a premonition that actually came true? Explain.

339. Have you ever served on jury duty? If so, what was the case about? If not, would you like to be on a jury in the future?

340. Did a sibling or childhood peer ever tease or torment you? Share the details.

341. What childhood accident stands out in your mind?

342. When the "tooth fairy" came, what did you usually get?

343. What's your favorite picnic memory?

344. Who was your least favorite teacher? Why?

345. Have you ever been let off the hook for a punishment you deserved? How did that make you feel?

346. Did you ever cheat on a school exam? Describe the situation.

347. What was a childhood disillusionment you experienced?

348. As a child, did you take music lessons or take part in band or choir? Explain.

349. What "close call" did you have from the past? Describe it.

350. What's the best advice you've ever been given?

351. How much trouble did you get into during your school days? Explain.

352. As a child, did you ever peek into a wrapped gift before you actually received it? Did you ever get caught? Explain the details.

353. What dream has come true for you?

354. What's one of the biggest purchases you made, and how did you negotiate the transaction?

355. What is your earliest childhood memory?

356. What nightmare woke you up in a panic?

357. How has your birth order affected you?

358. Have you ever suggested an idea for change that was adopted? What was it?

359. What's the best prank you've ever pulled off?

360. What's the best prank someone pulled on you?

361. Growing up, for the most part, were you respectful or disrespectful to your parents? Explain.

362. What lasting lesson did you learn from your parents?

363. What was the last concert you attended? Who did you go with?

364. What one new thing did you learn in the last week?

365. How many foreign countries have you visited? Which one stands out in your memory?

366. How many American states have you visited in your lifetime? Which was your favorite and why?

367. What has frustrated you in the recent past? Explain.

368. In what sports, clubs, or activities were you most involved during high school?

369. Who was your first boyfriend or girlfriend? What was he or she like?

370. What is the first movie you saw in a theater?

371. What was the name of your first album/CD?

372. What's something that you did growing up that your parents never found out about?

373. When were you in a situation where something struck you as funny, but it was inappropriate to laugh? What did you do to suppress your laughter? Explain the situation.

374. What's a favorite memory with your grand-parents?

375. "Life is not measured by the number of breaths you take, but by the moments that take your breath away" (George Carlin). When have you had such a moment?

376. When were you in a hospital? Describe the situation.

377. Have you (or someone you know) ever been on national television? Describe the situation.

378. Have you ever participated in a long distance walking, running, or biking event? Tell your story.

379. How many times did you move growing up? Describe your experience and how it impacted you.

380. What's the worst weather situation you've been in? Explain.

381. How would you describe your most magical childhood moment?

382. How would you summarize the highs and lows of this past week?

383. What was your best or worst job interview?

384. Have you ever had a challenging roommate situation? What was difficult about it?

385. What was your worst "nightmare" date?

386. What was your most romantic date?

387. What event in your life has brought about the greatest life-change?

388. What was one of your most frightening moments?

389. Was there ever a time when you or someone you know was a victim of fraud? Explain.

390. What was the best or worst job you ever had?

391. What outside influences have had the greatest impact on your family?

392. What's the best thing you ever built or created?

393. What's the story behind a time when a car you were in broke down?

394. What's the most adventurous or daring thing you have ever done?

395. What are your best or worst childhood memories of going to a zoo or circus?

396. What was a recent déjà vu experience?

397. Did you ever learn to swim? If so, how did you learn? Describe your experience.

398. How would you describe one of your happiest childhood memories?

399. What lesson did you have to learn the hard way?

400. When did you last have fresh flowers in your home? What was the occasion?

JUST
IMAGINE

401. If you could be invisible for a day, what would you do?

402. If you could eliminate one weakness or limitation in your life, what would it be?

403. If you could change anything about your relationship with your parents, what would it be?

404. If you could switch job responsibilities with your boss, would you do it? Why or why not?

405. If you were able to retrieve only one item on the way out of your burning home, what would that be? Explain.

406. If you could go back in time, what year would you visit? Why?

407. If you could go anywhere for a one-day visit, where would you go? Why?

408. If you could spend one hour doing absolutely anything, what would you do?

409. If you had the opportunity to travel into space, would you go? Why or why not?

410. If you had an unlimited shopping spree at only one store, which one would you choose? Why?

411. If you could play any instrument, what would you choose? Why?

412. If you could talk with only one person for the rest of your life, who would it be and why?

413. If you could visit with any person in history, who would it be and why?

414. If you could do something very daring without fear, what would you do?

415. If you could take an early retirement, what would you do?

416. If you had the chance to go anywhere for dinner tomorrow, where would you go? Why?

417. If you were assured you would not fail, what endeavor would you attempt?

418. If you could be any celebrity, who would you want to become? Why?

419. If you won a million dollars in the lottery, how would you spend it?

420. If you had to perform a "Stupid Human Trick" for the David Letterman show, what would you do?

421. If you could learn to speak a foreign language, which one would you choose and why?

422. If you could change one thing about your appearance, what would it be?

423. If you could change one thing about your personality, how would you be different?

424. If you were stranded on a deserted island, what three "luxury items" would you most want to have with you?

425. If you could rule the world for one day, what would you do?

426. If you could change your occupation, what would you do?

427. If you could give one gift to your children, what would it be?

428. If you could live anywhere in the world, where would it be?

429. If you were able to listen to only one music CD ever again, what would it be and why?

430. If you were to write a book about your life, what would it be called?

431. If you were imprisoned and were allowed only one book to read, what would you choose and why?

432. If you could restore one broken relationship, which one would you choose? Why?

433. If you could bring one person back from the dead, who would you bring back? Why?

434. If you could live your life all over again, would you? Explain.

435. If you could possess it, what superhero's super power would you want to have and why?

436. If you had to change your first name, what name would you choose?

437. If you had the opportunity to start your own business, what would you start? Why?

438. If you could cure a disease or heal a sickness, which one would you choose? Why?

439. If you could bring peace to one country, which one would you select? Why?

440. If you could look into the future to find out one thing, what would you want to know?

441. If you could relive any year, what year would you choose? Why?

442. If you could have invented one thing, what would it have been?

443. If you could develop something that's not been invented yet, what would you invent?

444. If you were a WWE Smackdown champion wrestler, what would be your name and calling card?

445. If there were no animals in our world, what would we be missing?

446. If you were a master sculptor for a day, what would you sculpt?

447. If you were offered free cosmetic surgery by the best plastic surgeons in the world, would you take it? Explain.

448. If you could rob from the rich and give to the poor and get away with it, would you do it? Why?

449. If you could rid the world of one evil, which one would it be? Why?

450. If you were stranded on a deserted island, which three people would you most want to have join you?

451. If you could own any sports team, which one would it be?

452. If you had the ability to compete in the Olympics, what event would you want to be in?

453. If you had the talent to play a professional sport, which one would you select?

454. If you could establish one charitable organization, what would it be?

455. If you could turn into any animal at will, which one would you select? Why?

456. If you could read everyone's mind for one week only, would you tell anyone or keep it a secret? Explain.

457. If you could be a radio or television personality, what kind of program would you choose?

458. If you were in charge of ending world hunger, where would you start?

459. If you had the time to volunteer for any worthwhile organization, which one would you choose? Why?

460. If you had to design a float for a parade, what would you design?

461. If you could live forever on earth, would you choose to do so? Explain.

462. If you were to paint a picture of your child-hood, what colors would you use? Describe your picture.

463. If you were on a debate team, what subject would you relish debating?

464. If you could rid the world of one fear, what fear would it be? Why?

465. If you could write a best-selling book, what would you write about?

466. If you were a doctor, which field of medicine would you specialize in? Why?

467. If you could change one thing about the culture you live in, what would it be? Why?

468. If you were required to distribute a million dollars any way you wanted, how would you do it?

469. If you were to star in a movie, what would be your ideal role?

470. If you could rewrite history, what one thing would you change?

471. If you were forced to give up one of your five senses, which one would you choose? Why?

472. If you had to choose right now, who would you select to be in your wedding party?

473. If you were a gifted painter, what picture would you want to paint first?

474. If you could give some advice to all parents, what would you say?

475. If you had to do your life over, what one thing would you do differently? Explain.

476. If you could be any cartoon character, which one would you be?

477. If you could make any improvement on how cars operate, what would it be?

478. If you could teach any class on any subject, what would you teach and to whom would you teach it?

479. If you could wave a magic wand and stop any one thing, what would you stop? Why?

480. If you could ask any question of the people you're with right now and get an honest answer, what question would you ask?

481. If you could trade places with anyone for one week, who would you want to trade with and why?

482. If you could make one character from any work of fiction come to life, what character would you select?

483. If you were a great explorer, what would you explore?

484. If you could be a contestant on any game show, which one would it be?

485. If you found an abandoned car with $50,000 in the back seat, what would you do?

486. If you could own a restaurant, what kind would it be?

487. If you could run Hollywood, what would you do?

488. If you could transport yourself at will between any two destinations, which two would you choose? Why?

489. If you could redecorate your home at no cost, what would you wish to do?

490. If you could be any age for the rest of your life, what age would you choose? Why?

491. If you could capture any event in history on videotape, which one event would it be?

492. If you were to get a tattoo, what would it be? And where would you put it?

493. If you could grant any three wishes to one person, to whom would you grant them? Why?

494. If you were going to a costume party next week, what costume would you wear?

495. If you could take back something you've said, what would it be?

496. If you were to fast-forward your life five years, where would you be and what would you be doing? What changes would people see in you?

497. If you could say anything to the people you're with right now, what would you say?

498. If you were given $100,000 to celebrate some-
one or something, who or what would you
celebrate?

499. If you could give one piece of advice to pass
on to the next generation, what would it be?

500. If you could hang a motto in every home,
what would it say?

VIEWPOINTS

501. What does "success" mean to you?

502. Do you think there will ever be world peace? Why or why not?

503. What's the secret to a long life?

504. Which is the greater tragedy: an innocent person imprisoned or a guilty person set free? Explain.

505. How important is it to set personal goals?

506. Are people trustworthy? Explain your answer.

507. What is beauty?

508. Why do you think people live in denial?

509. What new law is needed to make the world a better place to live?

510. How would you describe the perfect day?

511. In your opinion, what is the moral condition of this world?

512. Why do you think divorce is so prevalent?

513. What is the ideal age to get married? Why?

514. To what extent is knowledge power, to what extent is truth power, and what's the difference?

515. Do you believe that the human soul is eternal?

516. What is the greatest invention the world has ever seen?

517. What do you think is needed to make the world a better place?

518. What advice can you give about how to conquer fear?

519. What advice can you give about how to relieve stress?

520. Why are some people cruel and unkind?

521. What is the difference between knowing a lot of facts about a person and knowing someone personally?

522. What do you think is the secret to a happy marriage?

523. Why do innocent people suffer?

524. Why do bad things happen to good people?

525. Do you believe that, for the most part, people are basically good, basically bad, or a mixture? Why?

526. Is seeking truth a way of life or a season of life? Explain.

527. Do you believe ignorance is bliss? Why or why not?

528. Why do you think it's so hard for people to say they're sorry?

529. When does the end justify the means?

530. What do you think is the greatest problem of the human race?

531. Why are bad habits so hard to break?

532. Whom do you consider the greatest president of all time? Why?

533. What is truth?

534. What's more important, a healthy mind or a healthy body? Why?

535. What makes a true friendship?

536. Does life imitate art or does art imitate life? Explain.

537. What is "unconditional forgiveness"?

538. To what extent is it possible to show respect or tolerance and still disagree?

539. What does it mean when two people are said to have "chemistry"?

540. Do you think science will offer the "final answer" to all the world's problems? Why or why not?

541. To what extent is cloning a moral issue? Explain.

542. When is it better to be safe than sorry?

543. What does it mean to be powerful?

544. What is the benefit of meditation?

545. Why is it sometimes hard to forgive others?

546. What's most intriguing about the Cinderella story?

547. How well do you receive criticism from others? Why do most people fear honest feedback and evaluation?

548. What does this quote mean? "He is no fool who gives what he cannot keep, to gain what he cannot lose." (Jim Elliot)

549. What's the best approach for resolving conflict?

550. Which is more important: what you say or how you say it? Explain your answer.

551. Do you think a sixth sense exists? Explain.

552. Do you think the end or the means is most important? Explain.

553. When is it appropriate to resort to making a threat? When is a threat not a threat?

554. What role does trust play in our everyday relationships?

555. What's the best way to earn another person's respect?

556. When is it necessary to take the law into your own hands?

557. What is the basis of your standard of right and wrong?

558. What's the best way to win back an estranged friend?

559. What's the best way to resist peer pressure?

560. Which is greater, love of one's parents, one's children, one's spouse, or one's friends? Explain your answer.

561. What do you think is the most significant event in the history of the human race? Explain.

562. How would you define "freedom"?

563. What are the best ways to inspire or motivate people?

564. What's the best way to delegate things to others?

565. In raising children, do you think it's best to discipline by giving timeouts, discussions, spankings, or a combination? Why?

566. What's the best way to negotiate a raise in salary?

567. Where do you draw the line between helping people and showing them how to help themselves? How do you strike that balance?

568. What's a sure way to detect when someone is lying?

569. How do you measure contentment?

570. Why do some people resist living lives of moral integrity?

571. What's the best way to handle another person's hostility and ease tensions?

572. How important is physical appearance when it comes to achieving success or getting one's way in life?

573. Is cloning a sign of progress? Why or why not?

574. What's the age of accountability?

575. What is the secret to being content in all circumstances?

576. Who's the greatest leader of all time? Why?

577. Does work really banish three great evils—boredom, vice, and poverty? Explain.

578. What do you recommend to overcome self-pity?

579. If you did something wrong, would it make any difference that you did so unintentionally? Would you still be morally responsible? Explain.

580. How do you define "true love"?

581. What's the best approach to use in negotiating a fair purchase price for a car?

582. How do you suggest overcoming negative self-talk?

583. Why is it taboo to discuss personal financial matters?

584. What's the best remedy for anxiety caused by speaking in front of a large group of people?

585. When is failure a success?

586. Is there such a thing as a "just war"? Explain.

587. What's your position on capital punishment?

588. What is the meaning of life?

589. Why is life so hard? Why is life so complicated?

590. What's unforgivable?

591. If accumulation of money doesn't bring lasting happiness, what does?

592. Why are people who win the lottery often unhappier than they were before their win?

593. What happens after death?

594. What is it about human nature that tends to stubbornly refuse the aid of someone else?

595. What is the difference between an intellectual assent to a set of beliefs and an actual acceptance of those beliefs?

596. What purpose do the emotions of regret, shame, or guilt serve?

597. Do you think religious holidays have become too commercialized by society? Why or why not?

598. Do you think the general population is better off or worse off than it was fifty years ago? Why?

599. What's the difference between intelligence and wisdom?

600. What's one thing you know for sure?

HARD-HITTING

601. What's one regret you live with?

602. What do you live in denial about?

603. What phobias have you struggled with?

604. How difficult is it for you to forgive someone who refuses to apologize?

605. What's the most serious illness or injury you ever faced?

606. How are you different now than you were before September 11, 2001?

607. How would you prefer to die—quickly without warning or slowly over time?

608. What insults your intelligence?

609. What's one conviction you hold that you would be willing to die for?

610. When is it okay to lie?

611. What's your most embarrassing moment?

612. When have you had to agree to disagree? Explain.

613. What bad habit have you broken?

614. In an emergency, which friends would you feel the freedom to call in the middle of the night?

615. Where are you going?

616. What impossible task are you facing right now?

617. What fear are you trying to overcome?

618. Would most people describe you as humble or proud? Why?

619. Have you ever violated a confidence? Describe what happened.

620. Have you ever been falsely accused? Describe the situation and how you felt about it.

621. What character trait are you currently trying to improve or change?

622. Have you ever gotten caught doing something you shouldn't have done? Describe the occasion.

623. Was there ever a time when you were very sure of something, but were later proved wrong? Explain what happened and how you reacted.

624. If you just found out you had only two weeks to live, what top two or three things would you do? Why?

625. What do you suspect people say about you behind your back?

626. How have you been humbled? Describe the details.

627. When was the last time you said, "It's my fault—I'm sorry"? Explain the situation.

628. What scares you the most about the future?

629. What hot topic usually turns into an argument with you?

630. In what situation do you often find yourself "walking on eggshells"?

631. What traumatic event has changed your life forever?

632. Who's the "black sheep" of your family? Explain the situation.

633. What one person in your life do you find the most challenging? Explain.

634. What temptation have you successfully resisted? Describe the situation.

635. What's something about you that no one knows?

636. How do you comfort those who have suffered a tragedy or loss?

637. How difficult is it for you to speak the truth, even when it may be hurtful or unpopular?

638. What was the hardest era of your life?

639. Have you found your place in this world? If so, where is it?

640. If you died today, who would give your eulogy, and what would be said?

641. What one thing do you fear more than anything else?

642. How afraid of dying are you? Explain.

643. What's something for which you would seek revenge?

644. What was your last argument about?

645. How often do you tell little white lies? Give an example.

646. What is your greatest weakness?

647. How do you explain death?

648. What epitaph would you want engraved on your tombstone?

649. What kinds of things do you catch yourself exaggerating about?

650. What lie did you tell today?

651. Have you ever felt like you were taking three steps forward but two steps back? Explain.

652. What's the closest you've come to having an epiphany?

653. What would make you totally content right now?

654. What is something that you failed at?

655. What mystery have you solved?

656. When you think of really living and not merely existing, what comes to mind?

657. What's something you consider too daring to try?

658. How at peace are you with yourself? Explain.

659. Would you want to know the date and cause of your death? How would that information change things for you?

660. What is the hardest thing you've ever done?

661. What do you think is your purpose in life?

662. What's the most ridiculous thing you've ever stolen? Explain the situation.

663. What paradox (or contradiction) in life have you had to learn to accept or embrace?

664. To what extent are you an argumentative person? Explain.

665. Why are we here?

666. To what extent do you trust people? Explain.

667. Would you ever give up your life for a friend or family member? Why or why not?

668. If you knew your death could save a stranger's life, would you give up your life? Why or why not?

669. What do you hope to discover beyond the grave?

670. What lesson has failure taught you?

671. Is your "glass" usually half full or half empty? Why?

672. What's the most significant loss you've experienced?

673. What's the closest you've ever come to thinking you didn't deserve to live? Explain.

674. What's an example of your passive-aggressive side?

675. How do you know this world is not a dream? Can you prove it?

676. Have you forgiven yourself for past personal failures? Why or why not?

677. In what area of your life are you immature?

678. How do you deal with very needy people?

679. How do you most want to be remembered?

680. Did you ever witness someone die? Describe your thoughts and feelings at that time.

681. What important competition have you lost?

682. What do you hope will be your biggest life-time contribution to society?

683. What do you do to get "centered"?

684. Have you ever broken or spilled something in someone else's home? Did you try to cover it up or fix it so it would go unnoticed? Explain.

685. How healthy or unhealthy are you with setting boundaries? Explain.

686. "I do what I don't want to do and I don't do what I want to do." To what extent do you relate to that statement? Explain.

687. Do you ever fear "living" as much as "dying"? Explain.

688. Was there ever a time when your blood "ran cold?" Explain.

689. How have you dealt with loss in your life?

690. Is there such a thing as "destiny"? Why or why not?

691. How would you graciously turn down an invitation to go out on a date? How would you graciously break up with someone you were dating?

692. What positives, if any, have resulted from the suffering you've experienced in your life?

693. How do you deal with doubt?

694. What holds you back?

695. What negative behavioral pattern has been passed down from generation to generation within your family?

696. What brings out your pessimistic side?

697. What's missing in your life? What one thing would make your life complete?

698. How convinced are you that the sun will rise tomorrow? What makes you so sure?

699. Who are you when no one's looking?

700. How hard is life? How does your life compare?

FROM THE HEART

701. When was the last time you cried? Why?

702. How would you describe a time when you felt alone in a crowd?

703. What makes you stand to your feet and cheer?

704. On a scale from 1 to 10, how happy do you usually feel? Explain.

705. What's your most prized or sentimental possession? Explain.

706. What or who inspires you to be all that you can be?

707. When have you been overwhelmed with compassion or overcome with pity? How were you transformed by the experience?

708. What in this world breaks your heart?

709. If you had to locate the feeling of "longing" or "yearning" in your body, where would you say it was?

710. Describe a time when you lost something very valuable. How did you feel when you finally found it or when you realized it would never be found?

711. How do you handle anger?

712. What stresses you out?

713. What is something that always brings a smile to your face?

714. What mood are you usually in? Explain why.

715. What silly thing have you done in the name of love?

716. When was the last time you helped someone in need? Describe it.

717. What's one accomplishment that gives you great satisfaction?

718. What was your proudest moment?

719. In relationships, are you more often the "heartbreaker" or the "heart broken"? Why?

720. How many times have you really been in love?

721. How many times have you had a broken heart?

722. Whom have you lost touch with but still wonder about?

723. How have you honored your parents?

724. What's the most cowardly thing you've ever done?

725. Who has loved you more than anyone else in your life?

726. What was the happiest era of your life?

727. What's the most courageous thing you've ever done?

728. When have you recently felt overwhelmed? Describe the situation.

729. What one thing do you wish for more than anything else?

730. What do you dream about most often? How do you interpret your dreams?

731. What's the best greeting card you ever received?

732. How have you significantly honored another person?

733. What has recently made you depressed?

734. Have you ever felt excluded? Explain the situation and how it made you feel.

735. What was the best surprise you've ever pulled off?

736. What was the best news you've ever received?

737. When did you ever immediately "click" with someone you just met? What was the long-term result? To what do you attribute that kind of connection?

738. Was there ever a time when you were in need and someone met that need? Describe.

739. Is it better to have loved and lost or never to have loved at all? Explain.

740. What prevents you from revealing your emotions to others? Give an example.

741. What brings a tear to your eye?

742. When do you find yourself singing?

743. What color describes your mood right now?

744. Is there a family tradition that has a special meaning for you? Describe it.

745. Of the following ways, how do you most like to express your love to another person: touch, words, gifts, time spent together, or acts of kindness?

746. Of the following ways, how do you most like to receive expressions of love: touch, words, gifts, time spent together, or acts of kindness?

747. When do you feel the loneliest?

748. What makes you feel like pulling the covers back over your head and staying hidden in bed all day long?

749. What brings out your critical side?

750. What fuels you?

751. What poem or song really moves you? Share a line from it.

752. What's one thing that makes you really angry? Explain.

753. From what do you secretly long to be "rescued"?

754. What do you need to feel secure?

755. What was the greatest day of your life?

756. When you feel sad, what do you do to find comfort?

757. What objects from your childhood have you saved? Explain why.

758. Are you ever satisfied? Why or why not?

759. Do you use the word "love" freely and often or selectively and seldom? Explain why.

760. What's weighing heavy on your heart these days?

761. What do you do when a homeless person asks you for money? How do you feel afterward?

762. When you are happy, how do you like to celebrate?

763. How self-centered are you?

764. When have you had a cathartic experience and what was the impetus?

765. Is it better to love or be loved? Why?

766. Do you believe in "love at first sight"? Why or why not?

767. Do you believe in "soul mates"? Why or why not?

768. How is your love for your friends different from your love for your family?

769. What recent disappointment have you had?

770. When is the right time to demonstrate "tough love"?

771. Is there someone in your life who has never (or rarely) let you down? How long have you known this person?

772. When do you feel insecure?

773. To what extent do you trust your own judgment or gut instincts? Why?

774. What worries you?

775. How do you heal a broken heart?

776. Who have you loved more than anyone else in your life? Explain.

777. What do you want?

778. When was the last time your heart skipped a beat? Describe the situation.

779. When have you felt like you could "never repay" someone? Explain.

780. What does silence feel like to you?

781. What makes you feel jealous?

782. When was the last time your heart was in your throat? Describe the situation.

783. Was there ever a time when someone rescued you? Describe the closest thing that comes to mind.

784. Was there ever a time when you gave your heart completely over to something or someone? Describe the closest thing that comes to mind.

785. How often do you second-guess yourself? Why?

786. What situations cause you to hold back and protect your heart?

787. Have you ever felt like there was no escape; that your heart was trapped? Describe.

788. When have you felt betrayed?

789. What's your most cherished romantic moment?

790. What fills your heart up to the bursting level?

791. When do you feel out of control?

792. Has your heart ever lied to you, or do you think it always "tells" the truth? Explain.

793. When was a time when you felt honored? Describe the situation.

794. How often or easily do movies make you cry?

795. What's one question you are asking yourself these days?

796. Growing up, what virtue did you see in your parents that you hope to emulate?

797. How sensitive a person are you? Explain.

798. What part of your heart has never been seen by anyone? Why?

799. Have you ever had someone do something for you or give something to you that you did not earn or deserve? Describe the situation and how it made you feel.

800. What makes your heart beat fast?

SPIRITUALLY
SPEAKING

801. Why do you think there are so many different religions in the world?

802. Do you think that all the major religions are fundamentally the same or different? Explain your answer.

803. Do you think religion is an emotional crutch for some people? Why or why not?

804. What do you think heaven is like?

805. What do you think most people think about the Bible?

806. What do you think are the most common misconceptions people have about God?

807. Do you believe the Bible is actually God's chosen tool for communication to mankind? Why or why not?

808. Do you believe in reincarnation? Why or why not?

809. What do you like most about church, synagogue, or mosque?

810. Why does God seem so distant?

811. Do you think most people are spiritually attuned or spiritually ignorant?

812. What is your attitude toward people who believe differently than you?

813. Do you think God exists? Why or why not?

814. If God did not exist, what practical difference would that make in our world?

815. Is God dead? Explain.

816. Why do you think some people are skeptical about the existence of God? Why are others so certain he does exist?

817. Is belief in God intellectual suicide? Why or why not?

818. Do you think it's possible for anyone to know for sure if there is a God? Explain.

819. Why do you think that some form of religious belief is present in virtually every culture?

820. What do you like least about religion?

821. Do you think religion is necessary? Why or why not?

822. What are some characteristics you have heard taught about God that you do not believe?

823. Do you think religion should be a private matter? Why or why not?

824. Do you believe in miracles? Why or why not?

825. Do you believe God is actively involved in our world or detached and distant from our world? Explain.

826. How reliable do you think the Bible is as a historical document? Explain.

827. How would you explain eternity?

828. How many different religions have you studied in your lifetime, and which one makes the most sense to you right now? Explain.

829. Do you believe in an afterlife? Why or why not?

830. How do you think the afterlife will be different from this life?

831. How do you "remember your spirit"?

832. What does "being spiritual" mean to you?

833. Do you think most, if not all, wars would cease if no religious differences existed? Why or why not?

834. Are natural disasters God's doing? Explain.

835. How often do most people you know think about spiritual issues? Explain your answer.

836. If God decided to visit the planet right now, what do you think he would say or do?

837. Why do you think there are so many disagreements over spiritual and religious matters?

838. How do you picture the face of God?

839. Is your image of God more like that of a "grandfather," a "policeman," or a "mechanic"? Explain.

840. What's the central difference between psychology and religion, or do they address the same need in mankind? Explain.

841. What about God do you hope is true? Why?

842. What's the difference between being moral and being spiritual?

843. Do you think that scientific discoveries will eventually eliminate mankind's "need" for God? Why or why not?

844. What's the greatest spiritual advice you have ever received?

845. Given the pros and cons associated with deeply held religious beliefs, do you think that "religion" overall is a positive or a negative thing?

846. Do you believe that a spiritual realm exists outside of what can be perceived by the five senses? Why or why not?

847. How would you define "faith"?

848. Should faith in God be "blind" or should it require evidence? Explain.

849. What does it mean to take a "leap of faith"? Have you ever taken one?

850. Do you believe it is possible to encounter God in a personal way? Why or why not?

851. What, if anything, is the Bible good for?

852. What determines how much trust you will place in a spiritual authority?

853. Do you think a person, in order to be a certain religion, must be converted into that religion, born into it, or both?

854. How much influence has your family heritage had on your ultimate religious beliefs? Explain.

855. What is it that bothers you the most about religious fanatics?

856. What are the positives and negatives of joining a small group to discuss spiritual issues?

857. What did you like and dislike about any church services you've experienced?

858. Why did God start it all?

859. If you could design your own church service, what would it look like?

860. How many different paths do you think there are to God? Explain.

861. What is the difference between "faith" and "religion"?

862. Why does merely talking about Christianity often muster up negative images and angry reactions?

863. Generally speaking, does Christianity, with its apparent emphasis on sin, hell, and judgment, dwell too much on the negative? Explain your answer.

864. What are the various ways people attempt to earn God's forgiveness or favor?

865. What is one thing you no longer believe about God that you believed when you were younger? What changed your mind?

866. What's one benefit the world has gained as a result of Jesus Christ's life and teaching ministry?

867. What's one benefit the world has gained as a result of Muhammad's life and teaching ministry?

868. What's one benefit the world has gained as a result of Buddha's life and teaching ministry?

869. What's your basis for deciding which, if any, religion is right for you?

870. Do you believe there is anything to the "power of prayer"? Explain.

871. From where does evil come?

872. Why is there so much evil in the world?

873. What do you think are some methods God uses to communicate to people?

874. Do you believe it's possible for people to communicate with the dead?

875. Do you believe an evil spiritual being, such as the Devil, exists? Why or why not?

876. What is it about the Bible that most confuses you?

877. What is your position concerning the concept of hell?

878. If God can do anything, can he make a rock so heavy he cannot lift it? Explain.

879. How good do you have to be to get into heaven?

880. Can a person know for sure that he or she is going to heaven? Why or why not?

881. Do you think all religions lead to God? Why or why not?

882. What's the difference between tolerance of all religions and validation of all religions?

883. Do you think that in order for one religion to be totally true, all other religions must be completely false? Explain.

884. Do you think that ultimately, no matter what we believe about God, we will all end up at the same place as long as we are sincere? Explain your answer.

885. If the world contained no religion, how might things be different?

886. How do you react to a religious person who attempts to prosclytize you?

887. How do you define a cult?

888. Can anyone know for sure that his or her religion is right? Explain.

889. What is your definition of a miracle?

890. If a bona fide miracle were to occur in your life, do you think that would convince you that some kind of intelligent Supreme Being exists? Why or why not?

891. Why do you think most people find it difficult, if not impossible, to believe in miracles?

892. Do you think angels and demons exist? Why or why not?

893. What do you think angels are like, and what is their function here on earth?

894. Do you believe you have a guardian angel?

895. What is the greatest commandment?

896. What is the greatest sin?

897. Why do some people become uncomfortable discussing spiritual matters?

898. What factors have most influenced your current beliefs about God?

899. What does God want from us?

900. If you could ask God to do any three things for you, and you knew he would do them, what would you ask him to do?

EXTREME
SPIRITUAL
MATTERS

901. When and how often do you pray? What motivates you to pray.

902. On a scale from 1 to 10, how close to God do you feel? Explain.

903. Rate the level of intensity you have about wanting to know God? Explain your answer.

904. If a dimmer switch could represent your understanding of Christianity, how bright would your light be?

905. Has there ever been a time you were convinced you received direction from God? Describe it.

906. How do you discern God's direction for your life?

907. How has your belief or disbelief in God affected your life?

908. What fears do you have about God?

909. What makes it difficult for you to trust God?

910. If you were to explain to a friend what it means to know God personally, what would you say?

911. With everything in this universe that could consume God's time and energy, how much do you think God really cares about what happens in your life?

912. What is your greatest fear about what you'd be like if God were leading your life?

913. Why doesn't God do something about evil and suffering?

914. When have you experienced a situation in which you believe God intervened? Describe it.

915. What is your reaction to the Bible's claim that Jesus is the only way to God?

916. What has been your biggest obstacle to spiritual growth?

917. Where are you in your spiritual journey?

918. Using the compartments of a car, how would you describe where God fits into your life (trunk, driver's seat, back seat, glove compartment, passenger seat, etc.)? Explain your answer.

919. What prevents you from taking steps on your spiritual journey now?

920. Who will be in heaven? Why?

921. If God were to step in and wipe out every trace of evil, what would that do to the human population? Where would that leave you?

922. When have you seen "hell" here on earth?

923. Why do you suppose God doesn't just eliminate Satan now?

924. Where was God when terrorists attacked the World Trade Center and the Pentagon?

925. If you were to die today, would you go to heaven? On what do you base your answer?

926. If you could prove beyond a reasonable doubt that God exists, do you think you would seek out a relationship with him?

927. If you believed in the God of the Bible, do you think it would impact the way you lived? Why or why not?

928. Have you ever had something you would call a "spiritual experience"? Describe the situation.

929. What religious issues are you struggling with these days?

930. What kinds of things do you pray about most frequently?

931. What personal religious experiences have had the most profound impact on you?

932. How certain are you that your current belief about God is correct? What would change that?

933. What do you think is the difference between a religious person who makes it into heaven and one who does not?

934. Do you think it is possible for a man to gain the whole world and yet lose his soul? Explain.

935. What does it mean to be made in the "image of God"?

936. What would you suggest would be the best way for God to show his love?

937. What's your favorite Bible verse and why?

938. What's the most reassuring Bible promise you know? Explain your answer.

939. Was there ever a time when you sincerely wanted to know God's will regarding a decision you needed to make? What was the outcome? Describe the situation.

940. What season are you currently in with regard to your spiritual life?

941. What surprises you most about Jesus Christ?

942. According to your understanding, how would you summarize the central message of Christianity?

943. What's something most of your friends don't know about your spiritual side?

944. What do you think God would say to you right now?

945. What do you think God will say to you when you die?

946. Why do you think Jesus was born? Why were you born?

947. What's one thing about the existence (or nonexistence) of God that scares you?

948. The Bible says, "God is love." What does that mean to you?

949. Who is Jesus Christ to you?

950. What's the first question you will have for God when you die?

951. Who's the closest thing to a spiritual mentor to you?

952. How has God demonstrated his love to you?

953. What has produced the greatest spiritual growth in your life?

954. Have you ever prayed a prayer of desperation? Describe the situation.

955. How have you been disillusioned by religion?

956. How comfortable are you discussing spiritual things with others?

957. How is it possible that the death of one (Jesus Christ) overcomes (forgives) the sins of many (the whole human race)?

958. Do you think it is possible to have a false sense of security about your eternal destiny? Explain.

959. What do you think it means to be "born again"? What's your knee-jerk reaction to this term?

960. Is there something spiritual missing in your life? Explain.

961. Do you agree with this statement: "Going to church doesn't make you a Christian any more than going to a garage makes you an automobile" (Billy Sunday)? Why or why not?

962. How would you define sin?

963. What are the repercussions of sin, if any?

964. Do you think it is possible to be indifferent or neutral toward God without offending him?

965. What is your biggest personal spiritual dilemma or challenge?

966. What do you think was the purpose of Jesus Christ's death?

967. What reasons do you think Christianity gives for its assertion that Jesus is the only way to God?

968. In what ways is the Christian life difficult or impossible to live?

969. How has God changed you?

970. What do you think God's attitude is toward you?

971. Do you think becoming a Christian is an ongoing process, something that happens at a specific point in time, or a combination of the two? Give reasons for your answer.

972. Why should God let you into heaven?

973. Do you think God has ever used pain and suffering to get your attention? If so, what was he trying to get across to you?

974. How confident are you about what will happen to you in the afterlife? Explain.

975. Do you have any fears about being wrong about your spiritual beliefs? Explain.

976. If you were face-to-face with Jesus, what would he say to you? Give a reason for your answer.

977. Can hell, God's justice, and God's love all be real at the same time? Explain your answer.

978. How comfortable would you feel about praying out loud with someone? Why?

979. How do you distinguish God's voice from your own thoughts?

980. What miracle do you wish God would perform right now?

981. What's one doubt you have regarding the existence of a Supreme Being?

982. What would Jesus do if he were in your shoes?

983. When have you experienced the closest thing to a miracle? Describe it.

984. If you were to identify someone as a Christian, what definitive factors would you look for to support that claim?

985. Have you ever meditated for spiritual purposes? If so, describe your experience.

986. Have you ever been baptized? What does the sacrament of baptism mean to you?

987. How do you "feed your spirit"?

988. What's the closest you've come to having an encounter with God? Describe it.

989. To what extent is your view of God influenced by your view of your father?

990. For what are you most thankful to God?

991. In your opinion, is the Christian message mostly "good news" or mostly "bad news"? Explain your response.

992. When was a prayer of yours answered? Tell about it.

993. How frequently, if ever, do you read the Bible? What motivates you to read the Bible?

994. What's one thing about God you don't understand?

995. Do you make comparisons with others on a spiritual level? Why or why not?

996. How would you describe your own moral condition?

997. Do you believe sin causes a gap between God and you? Why or why not?

998. Do you ever become angry with God when things go wrong? Why or why not?

999. Do you find it easy to ignore or avoid facing up to deep spiritual matters? Why or why not?

1000. In what ways do your religious beliefs impact the way you live your life?

1001. If you could ask God one question you knew he would answer right away, what would it be?

Willow Creek Association
Vision, Training, Resources for Prevailing Churches

This resource was created to serve you and to help you in building a local church that prevails!

Since 1992, the Willow Creek Association (WCA) has been linking like-minded, action-oriented churches with each other and with strategic vision, training, and resources. Now a worldwide network of over 6,400 churches from more than ninety denominations, the WCA works to equip Member Churches and others with the tools needed to build prevailing churches. Our desire is to inspire, equip, and encourage Christian leaders to build biblically functioning churches that reach increasing numbers of unchurched people, not just with innovations from Willow Creek Community Church in South Barrington, Illinois, but from any church in the world that has experienced God-given breakthroughs.

WILLOW CREEK CONFERENCES

Each year, thousands of local church leaders, staff and volunteers—from WCA Member Churches and others—attend one of our conferences or training events. Conferences offered on the Willow Creek campus in South Barrington, Illinois, include:

Prevailing Church Conference: Foundational training for staff and volunteers working to build a prevailing local church.
Prevailing Church Workshops: More than fifty strategic, day-long workshops covering seven topic areas that represent key characteristics of a prevailing church; offered twice each year.
Promiseland Conference: Children's ministries; infant through fifth grade.
Student Ministries Conference: Junior and senior high ministries.
Willow Creek Arts Conference: Vision and training for Christian artists using their gifts in the ministries of local churches.
Leadership Summit: Envisioning and equipping Christians with leadership gifts and responsibilities; broadcast live via satellite to eighteen cities across North America.
Contagious Evangelism Conference: Encouragement and training for churches and church leaders who want to be strategic in reaching lost people for Christ.
Small Groups Conference: Exploring how developing a church *of* small groups can play a vital role in developing authentic Christian community that leads to spiritual transformation.

PREVAILING CHURCH REGIONAL WORKSHOPS

Each year the WCA team leads several, two-day training events in select cities across the United States. Some twenty day-long workshops are offered in topic areas including leadership, next-generation ministries, small groups, arts and worship, evangelism, spiritual gifts, financial stewardship, and spiritual formation. These events make quality training more accessible and affordable to larger groups of staff and volunteers.

To find out more about Prevailing Church Regional Workshops, visit our website at www.willowcreek.com.

WILLOW CREEK RESOURCES™

Churches can look to Willow Creek Resources™ for a trusted channel of ministry tools in areas of leadership, evangelism, spiritual gifts, small groups, drama, contemporary music, financial stewardship, spiritual transformation, and more. For ordering information, call (800) 570-9812 or visit our website at www.willowcreek.com.

WCA MEMBERSHIP

Membership in the Willow Creek Association as well as attendance at WCA Conferences is for churches, ministries, and leaders who hold to a historic, orthodox understanding of biblical Christianity. The annual church membership fee of $249 provides substantial discounts for your entire team on all conferences and Willow Creek Resources, networking opportunities with other outreach-oriented churches, a bimonthly newsletter, a subscription to the *Defining Moments* monthly audio journal for leaders, and more.

Willow Creek Association
P.O. Box 3188, Barrington, IL 60011-3188
Phone: (800) 570-9812 or (847) 765-0070
Fax: (888) 922-0035 or (847) 765-5046
Web: www.willowcreek.com

Building Bridges of Trust
That Lead People to Christ

SEEKER SMALL GROUPS

Garry Poole

Knocking on strange doors, handing out tracts, initiating engineered conversations—is that really what evangelism is all about? If you and those in your church get uncomfortable at the mere mention of the "E" word, then *Seeker Small Groups* will shift your whole concept to something different than anything you've ever experienced.

Right now there's someone in your circle of influence who could respond positively to the gospel—if only they found a nonthreatening way to explore spiritual issues honestly with others. *Seeker Small Groups* shows you how to reach unbelievers through small groups that meet their needs and help them encounter Christ.

A seeker small group is facilitated by a Christian leader, but the group members are seekers. The format gives non-Christians a safe place to come with their questions, objections, and obstacles and discuss spiritual matters on a regular basis. *Seeker Small Groups* will show you just how powerful and effective the seeker small group concept really is.

From the nuts and bolts of launching a seeker's group to the vision and values that will nurture an ongoing dialogue, *Seeker Small Groups* offers a proven way to reach out to those who are searching for spiritual answers and point them to Christ.

"In this excellent new book, Garry Poole passes on the practical wisdom he has gained from over twenty-five years of experience leading small groups in an evangelistic setting. I learned a great deal from *Seeker Small Groups* and recommend it."

—Nicky Gumbel, Founder and Director, The Alpha Course

Softcover
ISBN 0-310-24233-9

Pick up a copy at your favorite bookstore!

GRAND RAPIDS, MICHIGAN 49530 USA

WWW.ZONDERVAN.COM

TOUGH QUESTIONS

Garry Poole and Judson Poling

"The profound insights and candor captured in these guides will sharpen your mind, soften your heart, and inspire you and the members of your group to find vital answers together."

Bill Hybels

This second edition of Tough Questions, designed for use in any small group setting, is ideal for use in seeker small groups. Based on more than five years of field-tested feedback, extensive revisions make this best-selling series easier to use and more appealing than ever for both participants and group leaders.

Softcover

How Does Anyone Know God Exists?
ISBN 0-310-24502-8

What Difference Does Jesus Make?
ISBN 0-310-24503-6

How Reliable Is the Bible?
ISBN 0-310-24504-4

How Could God Allow Suffering and Evil?
ISBN 0-310-24505-2

Don't All Religions Lead to God?
ISBN 0-310-24506-0

Do Science and the Bible Conflict?
ISBN 0-310-24507-9

Why Become a Christian?
ISBN 0-310-24508-7

Leader's Guide
ISBN 0-310-24509-5

Pick up a copy at your favorite bookstore!

ZONDERVAN™

GRAND RAPIDS, MICHIGAN 49530 USA

WWW.ZONDERVAN.COM

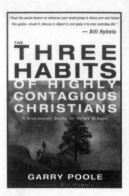